Listening In

Listening In

Lynley Edmeades

OTAGO UNIVERSITY PRESS
Te Whare Tā o Te Wānanga o Ōtākou

Published by Otago University Press
Level 1, 398 Cumberland Street
Dunedin, New Zealand
university.press@otago.ac.nz
www.otago.ac.nz/press

First published 2019
Copyright © Lynley Edmeades

Editor: Sue Wootton
Design/layout: Fiona Moffat
Back cover photograph: Rory Mearns

Cover: Paul Winstanley, *Interior 1*, 2003. Oil on linen, 900 x 710mm. Private collection.

Printed in New Zealand by Caxton

For Neil

Contents

This is the & of the world
—Caroline Bergvall

There is never nothing beneath something that is covered
—Deborah Levy

Calm and

In the distance he could hear
sound making a right go of it.
His lobes, with all their tucks
and echoes, were a cat's footsteps
on a wooden floor.
Together, they would make a bay
of calm and almost-static:
the sound moving out to ear,
his ear reaching out for hear.

Nodding is Soft

I can only tell you. What I saw.
And all I can. Say is that you.
Wouldn't have wanted. To see it
yourself no. Sir it was not.
For public. Consumption it was
very hard and very. Bad probably
the hardest and. Baddest thing
to see but yes. I saw. It I saw
it hard and it was. Bad but even
when I. Saw it I didn't say. Wow
that is the hardest. Thing I've ever
seen I just. Said when. Are we
leaving and you. Said well we
can leave when. You've finished
looking at the. Thing you're looking
at. And so I turned. Away but
already I. Knew it was. Not
worth telling you. About this
most hardest and. Baddest thing
it is not. Soft not like your. Nodding
is soft. But why are. You nodding
don't you know. That this is. The
hardest and baddest. Thing. No you.
Don't understand it is. The worst.

Where Would You Like to Sit

What brings you here today. Do you suffer from any long-term illness. Are you on any medication. What brings you here today. Are you in a long-term relationship. Are you on any medication. Have you done this kind of thing before. Are you in a long-term relationship. Do you worry about getting into debt. Have you done this kind of thing before. Do you often do things that are not to your advantage. Do you worry about getting into debt. Is it just the bank or do you feel indebted to people too. Do you often do things that are not to your advantage. What is your living situation like. Is it just the bank or do you feel indebted to people too. Do you often wish you'd grown up as a member of the opposite sex. What is your living situation like. Do you often think about changing your name. Do you often wish you'd grown up as a member of the opposite sex. Do you often feel guilty about things like that. Do you often think about changing your name. Do you imagine your life would be any different. Do you often feel guilty about things like that. Have you always wanted to speak another language. Do you imagine your life would be any different. Do you want a bigger life. Have you always wanted to speak another language. Do you often speak to strangers about your sex life. Do you want a bigger life. Do you prefer to think of desire as a finite emotion. Do you often speak to strangers about your sex life. Do you worry about how much alcohol you consume. Do you prefer to think of desire as a finite emotion. Why do you mistrust people who have never left their home towns. Do you worry about how much alcohol you consume. Do you think it is unusual for siblings to also be best friends. Why do you mistrust people who have never left their home towns. How often do you dream of wolves. Do you think it is unusual for siblings to also be best friends. Are you best friends with any of your siblings. How often do you dream of wolves. Have you ever thought about getting a pet. Are you best friends with any of your siblings. Do you suffer from a long-term illness. Have you ever thought about getting a pet. Where would you like to sit next time.

The Order of Things

Red tulips drooping in the park.
Remarkable how quickly things change.
It's tomorrow.
                    It's today.

Blue Planet Sky

Turrell Room, Kanazawa

Most of the time things slip

The seed on your plate slides
in the mess of leftover dressing

the hum of three street lights
making bright for no one

But every now and then
it feels as if things might hold

like here in this room
with its air and its airlight

as if the light has been washed
like the sky after a typhoon

We lie on the floor, grounded
by our great astonishment, the sky

so framed we almost understand
how it silences and blues

Look how the room renders
the real uncanny, Greg says

it makes of sky even more sky
so that all we see is verb

It is as if for a moment

For a moment it is as if

The Day
Cambrian Valley

The dog lies down in the shade of the table.
Knives lie down with pieces of lunch on them.
The mountains lie down across the valley
and the sunlight lies down across everything.

When we drive Neil says I love this:
the car and the music and the dog
and the sun and the spring and the lambs
and the light and the mountains and the sky.

The sky is so blue you can almost hear it skying.

Things to Do With Verbs

The day unravels in the precarious throws of verb.
It's everywhere we look: kitchen, bathroom, garden.
Even the floor waits in its doingness.

Later, when we've done all that was necessary
our doing has made little containers of past tense
around the house. We sit back and admire them
as they start their undoing, their done.

Things to Do With Day

Ad-libbing / agreeing / anticipating / arranging / asking
assembling / assuming / attempting / blinking / breathing
brushing / buying / calling / chewing / choosing / concluding
considering / consuming / contemplating / cooking
cooling / crunching / cutting / dancing / deodorising
digesting / distributing / dressing / drinking / drying
eating / emailing / ending / exposing / farting / feeding
feeling / filling / folding / frowning / gathering / going
greeting / gripping / guessing / hanging / holding
hugging / humming / imagining / inserting / interpreting
itching / joking / judging / laughing / leaning / licking
listening / looking / loving / marinating / masticating
masturbating / moisturising / nurturing / offering
opening / ordering / pausing / paying / picking / pissing
playing / posing / pouring / preparing / pressing / pushing
reading / rearranging / recognising / relaxing / reminiscing
researching / rising / rolling / rubbing / running / scoffing
seasoning / sharing / shitting / showering / singing / sitting
sleeping / slicing / slouching / smelling / sniffing / spelling
squeezing / standing / starting / stretching / sunbathing
swallowing / swimming / taking / talking / tapping
teasing / telling / texting / thanking / thinking / thrusting
tilting / touching / trying / turning / waiting / waking
walking / washing / watching / waving / wearing / wetting
wiping / wishing / wondering / writing / yawning.

Island

It's always yellow inside
and the nylon is an island
for the to and from the grass.

In the corner, some sand
from last summer's foot-stuck
and that forgotten sock.

Night makes a planetarium
of torch dust mosquito,
of hand toe torso.

Morning is gentle nose.
Sun on sleeping-bag-red
with the lurk of grass.

When the zipper goes
the yellow goes
to green, to blue

to day, to this
now, this now,
now this.

The Way

The way they met in Dublin and had hot, wet sex that very first night. The way they stayed in bed for two days, and then one morning, she took him to that pancake place, and told him she wanted to move to the other side of the world to be with him so that they could start a life together. Because of the way she just knew. The way he waited for her to come and when she said she was coming, he got the house ready. He waited until the neighbours had gone to bed before he reached his hand through the fence to steal some lavender to put on her side of the bed. The way he put on his best shirt and drove nervously to the airport. The way he apologised when they got back because the house was small and she said no, it's cute. The way they settled into a life. He would be there when she got home from work and would say hello darling, put your feet up, can I get you a glass of chardonnay. The way he'd make her laugh so hard she'd throw her head back and the way he felt that this special kind of laughter was reserved only for him. The way that made him feel, like he'd won the prize and the prize was her, and so one day he drove her to their favourite beach and asked her to marry him and then they ran away to a tropical island to get married and when they got back they had a big party with all their friends and everyone was so happy. He was happy too. The happiest he'd ever been. The way they did things that only very happy people do, like go to Paris to see their favourite band, or on a road trip through the desert. Or the way she secretly went back to that shop they'd been to in Rome and bought those shoes he'd fawned over, and then wrapped them up in that beautiful Italian paper for his birthday a few months later. He almost cried because no one had ever done anything so thoughtful for him before. Or the way that sometimes he would be worried about something and she would look at him as if to say everything is okay, and he could believe her because of the way she said it without saying it and because he trusted her in the way that makes you realise you've actually probably never trusted anyone before, which is both terrifying and a huge relief. The way they decided on things together, like getting a dog and what kind of dog and what to call the dog. Or not to have children, because of the way the planet is already bulging and the way they both felt that what they had was enough, what with all the laughter and the travelling and the dog and whatnot. But then the way she started to doubt things but didn't tell him because she thought the travelling and the dog might make the doubting go away. The way it didn't. The way it all happened so fast: that other man came along and the way she told him she was leaving, like it was no big deal, and then she left. The way he thought he'd never sleep again. The way they had to talk about selling the house and who was going to keep the dog. The way their friends would react, as if it was some kind of sick joke. The way that made it seem that nothing lasts forever, not even love, and that sometimes this is just the way that things pan out. The way that getting married used to be forever but the way that changed, too.

Indonesian Wedding
in memoriam

On the day of the wedding we woke up early.
There were six empty bottles of Bintang beside the door.
Everyone said good morning and how did you sleep
and wow, it's going to be an epic day.

It was warm.
The towels and bikinis had dried.
The locals were already in the shade.
The groom's gone for a surf, I heard someone say.

I wondered how we'd get through the day
with all its blaring radiance: too much for the living.
We could try spying on ourselves, I thought.
Make like dead people and watch the whole thing from above.

Chicken

You've been thinking that you should start answering your phone. So when your father calls, you do. You accept the call because you know from your mother that a friend of theirs has just died. I'm sorry to hear about Jenny, you say. I just can't get my head around it, he tells you. This makes you feel sad, in a where-are-the-words-for-this kind of way. You're cooking a chicken with a lemon shoved up its arse. We just had such a special connection, her and I, he says. You agree with him, and say things like yes, it must be so hard for you. Then while you're checking the chicken you wonder why you've never heard him talk about Jenny before. You stab the chicken and its juices ooze out to the edges of the oven tray. It's good to put a lemon up its bum, Jamie Oliver says. It stops the chicken from drying out. Nobody likes a dry chicken.

The Bee Elle

That man is annoyed
with that woman
for shuffling in her chair.
That woman has been staring
at that man for so long
that even I feel embarrassed.
Another woman was too busy
readwalking just now
to realise she had sat down
at someone else's desk.
I pretend not to see
when she looks around
for witnesses.

At lunchtime
we fill the mezzanine
with a wired sound for world,
hooked up to various elsewheres
as if our bodies don't matter.

Les Voisins

The man with the broken hip who walks
with his dog most days the woman with the garden

with the old plates she's used to line the edge
the bald guy who accidentally killed his own cat

by going up his own driveway too fast
the couple who live in an old converted shop

so use the footpath as their verandah and who
have just had a baby because she was pregnant

and now she's not and they sit on their verandah
and smoke and that must be when the baby is asleep

the woman who has two young boys but no husband
or partner and who seems to be finding things quite hard

but has just recently got a good load of firewood
and because of that and because the potatoes

out the front of her house are growing well
things might be looking up the teenagers

who have two La-Z-Boys facing the sun in the garden
who don't seem to care if they get wet

although they're never sitting in them the guy
with the collection of BMWs one that he drives

and some others that sit on the grass
beside the driving one the woman with the pink

hydrangeas the family with the broken window
and the tarpaulin that is trying to keep out the rain

but seems to be failing the couple who sometimes
yell at each other about the time she didn't pay him back

that fifteen dollars the woman who chases away other
people's cats with a wooden spoon the woman

who likes to walk around and watch everyone
when she thinks they're not looking.

L'Ordre des Things

Tulipes de rouge drooping in le parc.
Remarquable à quelle quickly les things changent.
C'est demain.
          C'est aujourd'hui.

The Age of Reason

Because longing
Because hormones
Because thirty-six
going on thirty-seven
Because psychotherapy
Because not understanding
Because antidepressants
Because New Zealand
Because domesticity
Because being scared
of enjoying domesticity
Because Simone de Beauvoir
Because money
Because *the best start*
Because not enough money
Because middle class
Because regret
Because my issues
Because potential regret
Because nieces and nephews
Because fear of death
Because a dog might do
Because antidepressants
Because déjà vu
Because the trees
Because the population
Because plastic
Because the ocean
Because everything
Because nothing
Because maybe
Because baby.

Like a Vase

All night the rain makes arc and noise
on vacant panes and the windows
keep themselves thickly poised
wetting into the corners like willows
and making borders with the dark.
When I wake I hear the damp
creeping in around the edges, the bark
of how it feels to wake in the camp

of what and how and when again.
I'd like to stay in bed, be soluble
when the days are floppy with possible,
have nothing on the confidence of rain.
Instead, my plans leak and my measures
are inaccurate, like a vase.

&

Loveliness Extreme

Here is your flask, now get inside—Sawako Nakayasu

You were, in all honesty, already focused on the possibility of loveliness—the way her hair kept lilt, even at the end of the day; the sound of the ordinary birds. Japan, people had told you, is a great place to buy pottery. Here, everything is lovely, and because it is, you're not sure how to deal with it. That is lovely, and those are extremely lovely, you hear yourself say, especially those pottery vases. The Japanese word for vase is *kabin*. They use *kabin* for ikebana, which is another extremely lovely thing. It even translates to a lovely thing: the way of the flower. Vase.

Extreme Loveliness

I would have liked more Japanese pieces in my vase collection
—James K. Baxter

Lovely, already focused on the pottery. Here, is another extremely lovely possibility of the way of the possibility of the ordinary birds. Japan, people have told you, is a great place. You hear *another hair kept lilt*, which translates to *buy pottery*. Here, even *in* is a lovely thing: the way of lovely, and because lovely, *kabin*. In Japan, people have told you, you're not sure how to buy pottery. Here, *in* is a great place, is lovely and is. They told you, already focused on the way her extreme loveliness is already focused on the way of the ordinary birds and the loveliness of. The pottery.

Extremely Love

Please don't put that vase in the dishwasher
—Abraham Lincoln

The pottery. You hear it said. Is extremely lovely, utsukushī in Japanese.
The Japanese is already ordinary birds. In all honesty is the way of the
way her extremely utsukushī and that is an utsukushī and this is a great
place. You can hear lovely extremely utsukushī, the way her
              hair kept lilt, which translates to buy pottery. Here
                             in is another extremely
        utsukushī
and because lovely, and because utsukushī, and because
        lovely lovely utsukushī utsukushī
then lovely utsukushī.
        Possibility of the way
            her
        extremely utsukushī, and because
                utsukushī
            is an
    utsukushī utsukushī
        utsukushī utsukushī utsukushī utsukushī,
            and
      because 美しい.

Thエ オrder オf Thイngs

レd チュlips drオ—ping イn thエ パrk.
レmarkable hオw quickリ thイngs チヤnge.
イt's ├morrow.
          イt's ├day.

Remainder

(1)
About the lights themselves, he can say very little.
Almost nothing.
They involve logistics and putting things in boxes.
Packing.
Things, stuff.
That's it really: all he can divulge.
Not much, I know.
It's not that he's being shy.
It's just that—well, for one, he doesn't even remember the house.
It's a blank: a white slate, a black hole.
He has vague images, half-impressions: of being, or having been—or more precisely,
    being about to be.
Blue light, railings, lights of other colours, being held above some kind of tray
    or bed.
But who's to say his imagination didn't just make them up?
Or pull them out from somewhere else, some other slot, and stick them there
    to plug the gap—the crater—that the lights had made?
Minds are versatile and wily things.
Real chancers.

(2)
About the chance itself, he can say very little.
Almost nothing.
It involves imagination and putting things in boxes.
Packing.
Things, stuff.
That's it really: all he can divulge.
Not much, I know.
It's not that he's being plastic.
It's just that—well, for one, he doesn't even remember the lights.
It's a blank: a green slate, a white hole.
He has vague lines, half-images: of being, or having been—or more precisely,
    being about to be.

Pink light, electric cords, lights of other colours, being helped above some kind
     of box or bed.
But who's to say his pondering didn't just make them up?
Or pull them out from somewhere else, some other window, and stick them
     there to plug the gap—the crater—that the lights had involved?
Minds are involved and wily things.
Real institutions.

(3)
About the institution itself, he can say very little.
Almost nothing.
It involved surplus and putting things in boxes.
Packing.
Lights, stuff.
That's it really: all he can present.
Not much, I know.
It's not that he's being carpet.
It's just that—well, for one, he doesn't even remember the floor.
It's a blank: a slate green, a hole white.
He has vague aspects, half-current: of being, or having been—or more precisely,
     being about to be.
White light, bought and sold, lights of other colours, being propelled above
     some kind of description or investment.
But who's to say that his handshake didn't just make them up?
Or pull them out from somewhere else, some other boardroom and stick them
     there to thumb the something—the crater—that the doorway had expected?
Minds are expected and chequered things.
Real diagrams.

(4)
About the diagram itself, he can say very little.
Almost nothing.
It involves openings and putting things in books.
Filing.
Lights, stuff.
That's it really: all he can sound.
Not much I know.

It's not that he's being vaporised.

It's just that—well, for one, he doesn't even remember the landscape.

It's a gloop: a white slate, a spider plant.

He has vague furnishings, half-woman: of being, or having been—or more
        precisely, being about to be.

Eventually light, bought and enough, lights of other plants, being blasted above
        some kind of kitchen or Portuguese.

But who's to say that his Annie didn't just make them up?

Or lush them out from somewhere else, some other courtyard and express
        them there to right the staff—the crater—that the panes had removed?

Minds are beautiful and wily things.

Real plants.

(5)

About the plant itself, he can say very little.

Almost nothing.

It involves cabins and engines and containing things in hubcaps.

Floating.

Lights, stuff.

That's it really: all he can phone.

Not much, I know.

It's not that he is being forensic.

It's just that—well, for one, he doesn't even remember the corner.

It's a grid: a Russian slate, a tingling piston.

He has vague firings, half-dipped: of being, or having been—or more precisely,
        being about to be.

Lamppost light, patterned and metal, lights of other times, being kicked past
        some kind of portion or pavement.

But who's to say that his BMW didn't just make them up?

Or drop them out from somewhere else, some other individual and stick them
        there to graph the driver—the crater—that the column had removed?

Minds are containing and wily things.

Real squares.

(6)
About the square itself, he can say very little.
Almost nothing.
It involves cheekbones and understanding and something something something.
Weights.
Lights, stuff.
That's it really: all he can repeat.
Not much, I know.
It's not that he's being answered.
It's just that—well, for one, he doesn't even remember the patient.
It's a prison: a breadstick slate, a straight white hair.
He has vague anger, half-something: of being, or having been—or more precisely,
    being about to be.
Husky light, working class and handsome, lights of other books, being this and
    that past some kinds of murderers and psychos.
But who's to say that his weights didn't just make them up?
Or repeat them out from somewhere else, some other assurance and stick them
    there to manage the thought—the crater—that the books had informed?
Minds are sparkling and wily things.
Real sausages.

The Dubious Structural Expressiveness of Arnaut Daniel
non-translated from the Occitan

Low from the valley-kill, score my entry—
the name partly goes back to consider all angles.
The lozenge is the key part of Mel's disarmer
and puss is no loss, but rub rum in the verge.
See vials of frown, lay them on your no-hooray uncle.
Choose to ride me, on virgins or on camera.

Can I solve the issue of the camera
on a Monday? Say quenelles are on entry
and my singing puts carefree in my uncle.
No, I am a member of the miscellaneous angle.
Aussies come feeling unfazed even on the verge.
Telford, I do not see a proper disarmer!

Decorate frost, not the armour
and consented maceration on camera.
Careless me has never crocheted atop a verger.
Carlos uses his layout as an illusory entry
and his doilies to sear capsicums on an angle.
A non-crier undermines your uncle.

And the error of my uncle
is in an age when titans request a disarmer,
when equating verses comes as a loaded dangle.
Sally's plague now grasses the camera,
semi-postwar llamas are a corn kernel entry.
Meals are soon welcome for the frivolous verges.

Put the fluoric lasses on the verge
and nude Adam on rebate as your uncle.
Tan the fixators in the sequel to your entry.
Concur that your fusing encore is not nice in armour

and on questioning the forcing plan of a tin camera.
Whisk your nosey part-doilies into a tent wrangle.

Also empyreans are even angles
when you amass cause in lieu of escorts on the verge.
Quilmes does enjoy terse play on camera
but give no name to parents; free your non-uncle.
Queen Paradise is Nora's double joy armour.
See how annuals hamper anomalous entry?

Arnaut tramples on your chanting dangling uncle
and Grant Desiree, he armours his own entry.
No cellist verges on a quelling camera.

Say Sibilance

Alison sensed some ladies used screen shots as surfaces.
She tells us to start listening, purposefully listening
so once self-contained sounds also suggest silences.
Steven's piece is circles. His seeing is constrained.
Listen: is Stein also whistling? Seems so.

She says socialising takes investment,
inseparably constellated institutions
across such vast visual scenes
separate as syntactical
so syntax is must.

Phaedrus himself
is strange.
So stand.
Ask. Preserve.
Silently question.

Is this
was,
is
this
once?

Witness
Stein
as sign
as us
as such.

Saying this
is this
same
as saying
Cindy Sherman?

Using some same songs
sky songs, as skies show promise
as is unnecessary, as necessary as Pocahontas
as necessary as she dances,
as so she always dances.

So dance, listen, dance.
Dance dance dance
dance dance
dance,
circle.

Circle is surface as fetish is circle,
as circle is circle as loose astonishing circle.
As house: whistling house, circling house
circling whistling housing house.
Realise linguistic inadequacy.

Some indigenous theorists say
this has distinctly considerable similarity
as juxtasupposition.
Oops: juxtaposition.
Is this post-structuralism?

This is spilling liveliness.
This displays such spills as fills
so this series is as discursive
as seeing modernism destabilise subjectivities
as descriptive scenarios. So stupid.

Yes, this is stupid.
This is as stupid as farts, says Ross.
Most useful philosophers understand farts.
Ross just sees Western uselessness.
Ionesco is against such essayists.

Some publishers publish useful essays.
Some publish useful stories.
Some publish useful poems.
Some publish useless poems.
Some poems stay useless always.

Some say yes.
Some say certainly.
Some say this is useful.
Some say this is useless.
Some say stop.

Ear Cleaning
an un–translation

Te frist (t)ask of te akustisk designer ist o learn now two (g)listen.
　　Ear cleaning is l'expression oui use hier.
Many excerises can be de vised to aide cleanse l'ears
　　but te most importante at frist are those which teach la whakarongo
to achtung silence.
　　This is especially importante in a bizzy, nerveux society.
Won exercise we often give our stew dents is to declare a
　　moratorium on speech for a full dag.
Stop making sownds for a while and eavesdrop ont hose made by
　　(m)others.
C'est a challenging and even frightening excerise and not everyun can
　　accomplish it, but those who do s(peak) of it après-wards
　　as a spécial event in there vies.

On (br)other occasions we prep are for (g)listening experiences avec
　　elaborate relaxation ou concentration excerise.
It mey take un heure of preparation in order to be able to (g)listen
　　clearaudibly to te neckst.

Sometimes it is useful to s(eek) out won sownd avec particular
　　charactéristiques.
For instance, try to find a sownd with a rîsing starting putch, or une
　　　　that consists of a series of petite nonperiodic bursts; try to find won
that makes a dull th(u)d followed by a high twítter;
　　or juan that combines a büzz and a squeæk.
Such sownds will not be fownd in every environment, of course, but
　　te (g)listener will be forced to inspect every sownd carefully in
　　te search.
Their are numeroneous (y)other excerise like this in mye music
　　edukation book lets.

Thuh Awrder uhv Things

Red tyoolips drooping in thuh pahrk.
Rimahrkuhbuhl hou kwiklee things cheynj.
Its tuhmawroh.
         Its tuhdey.

Speetch

Write how you speak—Louise Wallace

Mista speaka, I ryes to address this house for the viry last time. It's bin a huge privlidge to have servd the people of Hilinsville as thir mimber of parlamen, annov course the people of Newzillan as their pryminister. Evin though it was fifteen yeahs ago ah that th'time has past win I fist came here, in many ways it fils not that long ago that I rose to speak for the viry fist time withal the emoshuns this house canin voke. Excidement, tripidashun, fearan hope. This place is like no utha. Its all conshuming, life chinging, mostly powiful, occashunly trivial, but neva boring. Whatappens here matters a grate deal to the lives of milliuns of keewees who eviryday trustusas politishuns to geddit right on thir beharf. I came here onna diffrint path from many that had cum before me. I'd not beenna member of my pardies youth wing; in fact I haddin been thit involved withe nashnal party attall prior to throwing my hat in the ring for the silicshun of the Hilinsville seat. Although eyed always bin a nashnal supporta and proud ovit. Eyed not come here from a life of polltics and protest, in fact I came here from Wall Shtreet. But long before Wall Shtreet my politicul views hid been shaped by my Aushtrian Jewish mutha Ruth, who single handedly raised me and my sisstas in now the infimiss state house at nineteen Hollyfird Av Chrischurch. My mutha wazza no nonsense womin who refused to take no in inswer. She wuddun accept fayure. She was in imminsely hard worka, fistly as a night porta in the Claringdon Hotel so she cud earn money whyllow fimily slipt. Thin for miny yeahs she wurked azza cleaner, and evinin retirmint azza voluntear. She was offen ubrupt. Whileyes at high school, I hadda weekind job in sum stables anneye rimimber coming home one day it the age of fifteen to tell mum I hid this brillyunt idea. I was leaving school to train racehorses. No shesid. Shall we talkaboudit I inkwayered. No shesid. Not evin the prosand cons eye suggested. No shesid. You're going to universidy to stidy accounding. That wazzit. To mum, no ment no. I dun think she wuddive lasted viry long in coallishun govament, but thatsa by the by. Not thit she was always lost for words. Um, one day, earlyon in my fist job I bounced a chick. The bink miniger, he'ada vew on that, he wazza novice he shudda takin lessons from mum. Azzi sid she was offen ubrupt bit that day she wazzin full flight. Shid wurked hard all ov er adult life to make shure she paid her bilzon time and she expected thadder three childrin do the same. By nature eyema pragmatist noddan idealog. Thaz becos in my expiriunts most people jus wunt results thit work. Sum people have

48

sid that my pragmitizzim indicates the lack of clear site of principils. I don think thatshtrue. Itshjus that my principils derive mostly from the values and ithics instilled in me by my upbringing rither than the poltics wun oh wun texbook. Wunce wheneyesabout twelve I rither thoughtlessly asked my mutha ova dinna why iviry wun had nicer things than we did. Why they hadda bedda house than we had and how cum they wennon more holdays to more exciding places. For a momen mum was quite a taken bick. I'm doing my bist for you, she sid, I may not be able to give you what sum otha kids have bit I can give you my love and I can give you diterminashun.

Again America Great Make

a^{15} about^2 accept across^6 action^2 administration affairs again^{10} against aid airports all^{12} allegiance^2 alliances allowing almighty along alphabetize always^2 America^{19} American^{16} an^3 and^{75} another^2 anyone^2 anything are^{14} armies arrives *as*^{5} assembled at^5 back^5 be^{12} beautiful became because^2 become bedrock been^4 before^2 behind belongs^2 benefit Bible big bigger birth black bleed bless^2 blood body borders^3 born borne breath^2 bridges bring^4 brown build Bush but^{13} buy by^6 came can cannot capital^3 carnage carry Carter cash celebrate celebrated celebration center ceremony challenge challenges changes chief child children^2 cities citizens^4 city^2 civilized class Clinton closed come companies complaining completely confidence confront constantly controlled controls conviction cost countries^3 country^9 courage course creator crime crucial D.C. day^3 debate decades decay decision decree defend defended define *delivery* demands depletion deprived destiny^2 destroying determine Detroit did different disagreements disappeared disease disrepair divisions do^3 doing dollars done^2 down dream dreams^5 drugs each earth^2 education effort empty energies enforcement enjoy enriched entire eradicate establishment even^2 ever every^7 everyone^4 example exists^2 expense face^2 factories^3 fail fallen families^3 far fear fellow fight^2 fill finally first^3 flag flourished flush follow^2 for^{16} foreign^3 forever forget forgotten^2 form forward four free freedoms friendship from^{11} future gangs gather gathered get^2 giving glorious^2 God^4 going good^2 goodness goodwill govern government^3 gracious grateful great^7 group guide hall hands hardships harness has^6 have^5 heal hear heard heart^4 here^4 highways hire historic home homes honestly hopes horizon hour how however I^3 ignored immigration importantly impose in^{14} inauguration industries industry^2 infrastructure infused inner interests into is^{21} Islamic issuing it^{12} its^3 itself job^5 joined just justice knowledge labor lady land^2 landscape large law lead leaves left^3 let^3 life^2 lift like^3 likes line listening little live^2 living long^2 longer^2 look looking looks love loyalty^2 made^2 magnificent make^5 making many^3 match matters meaning men^2 merely Michelle middle military^2 millennium millions^3 minds miseries moment^3 most mothers mountain^2 movement^2 much must^3 my mysteries nation^{11} national^2 near Nebraska neighborhoods never^6 new^6 night no^6 not^9 now^9 oath^2 Obama^3 ocean^2 of^{47} off office old^2 on^7 one^9 only^2 open openly or^3 orderly other^5 our^{47} out over^2 overseas own^2 pain^2 part party^2 past patriotism patriots peaceful people^9 plains pleasant politicians^2 politics potential poverty power^4 prejudice *prepared* president^5 pride products promise prosper prospered prosperity protect protected[4] protection proud public pursue put radical railways rather ravages ready reality reaped reasonable rebuild rebuilding red rediscover redistributed refusing reinforce remember remembered restore rewards rich right[5] righteous ripped roads robbed Roberts room rulers rules rusted-out sad safe[2] salute same[5] scattered schools see seek[2] seen serve share[2] shine shores should shuttered sights simple sky small[2] so[3] soldiers solidarity souls space spacing speak special speech single spent spirit sprawl stand start starting states[2] stealing steps stir stolen stops[2] strength[2] striving strong struggling students subsidized success[2] system take talk[2] taxes technologies tell tells tens terrorism thank[2] that[8] the[68] their[11] themselves then[2] there[3] these[3] they[5] think this[10] thought thrive through throughout time[2] to[37] today[5] together[4] tombstones tomorrow too[3] total totally trade transfer transferring[2] transition trapped trillions triumphs[2] truly tunnels two understand understanding unite united[3] unity unlock unrealized unstoppable up upon urban us[2] very[2] victories[2] vision voice want was Washington[2] watching way[2] we[46] we've[3] wealth[4] welfare what[2] when[3] whether[3] which[4] while[6] white who will[40] windswept winning[2] wisdom with[8] women[2] wonderful words work workers[2] world[6] years[2] yes you[12] young your[11]

Ask a Woman

Where would you like to sit?
I am extraordinarily patient, provided I get my own way in the end.

What brings you here today?
If you want to cut your own throat, don't come to me for a bandage.

Do you suffer from any long-term illness?
To cure the British disease with socialism was like trying to cure leukemia
with leeches.

Are you on any medication?
One doesn't tell deliberate lies, but sometimes one has to be evasive.

Are you in a long-term relationship?
There is no such thing as society. There are individual men and women,
and there are families.

Have you done this kind of thing before?
You and I come by road or rail, but economists travel on infrastructure.

Do you worry about getting into debt?
Pennies do not come from heaven. They have to be earned here on earth.

Is it just the bank or do you feel indebted to people too?
The problem with socialism is that you eventually run out of other people's
money.

What is your living situation like?
A world without nuclear weapons would be less stable and more
dangerous for all of us.

Do you worry about how much alcohol you consume?
If you want something said, ask a man. If you want something done, ask a
woman.

Do you often do things that are not to your advantage?
To wear your heart on your sleeve isn't a very good plan; you should wear it inside, where it functions best.

Do you often think about changing your name?
I like Mr. Gorbachev.

Do you often wish you'd grown up as a member of the opposite sex?
The battle for women's rights has been largely won.

Do you often feel guilty about things like that?
I owe nothing to Women's Lib.

Do you imagine your life would be much different?
No one would remember the Good Samaritan if he'd only had good intentions; he had money as well.

Have you always wanted to speak another language?
It's a funny old world!

Do you often speak to strangers about your sex life?
It may be the cock that crows, but it is the hen that lays the eggs.

Do you prefer to think of desire as a finite emotion?
Look at a day when you are supremely satisfied at the end. It's not a day when you lounge around doing nothing; it's a day you've had everything to do and you've done it.

Why do you mistrust people who have never left their home towns?
Of course it's the same old story. Truth usually is the same old story.

Do you think it is unusual for siblings to also be best friends?
Standing in the middle of the road is very dangerous; you get knocked down by the traffic from both sides.

Are you best friends with any of your siblings?
Nothing is more obstinate than fashionable consensus.

How often do you dream about wolves?
I seem to smell the stench of appeasement in the air.

Have you thought about getting a pet?
Pandas and politicians are not happy omens.

Do you often want a bigger life?
What Britain needs is an iron lady.

From a Place Inside Where a Planet Grows

Hello!

Oh my. All those poems and now for the hard part. A cover letter. I am, well. One dear friend tells me I AM a poem. I often feel like one. I hope this is enough.

I love writing poetry and have done so alone in my bedroom, mostly late at night. I am 78 years old. I may not be a great writer, however I am prolific. Ten novels in two years. See my web page. I've been writing since I could hold a pencil. A ghost writer. Two books out with my name on the front. Never heard of them? Well hang on. Have I got a story for you.

This winter was hard. We had many visitors to the gardens to feed. Some real characters. The starlings stole the show with their sassy up-yours attitude, even when faced with the brutish bully fieldfares!

I will not bore you with further information about my hopes, dreams and aspirations. I am sure you are already most aware that I wish to be successful as a writer. Aside from that, I love all things involving tea or the moon. I can't stand the way most people pronounce 'for' in a sentence, somehow, it always becomes 'fur'. I've seen quite a bit of the world and cannot wait to see more of it. At the top of my Things To Do Before I Die list, you will find seeing a tow truck towing a tow truck. I feel it's good to have goals. I've also made a list of all the things that annoy me. My goal is to use it to annoy other people. Then it would be like the tow truck.

I am a product of opposites, and an immigrant on these celestial shores.

Today I chose the letter W. Why W, you may ask? Well, the W stands for Win. Like in the example, I will WIN the money. What else?

I'm finding poetry so much fun even when I am in the midst of mild depression and severe anxiety, lol.

I firmly believe that the mud and air from where we are born fuses with our blood and our bones, creating that instinct for home.

I like to dig into ethical and metaphysical questions and make music with syllables.

I eat, sleep and breathe poetry.

I believe! I believe we are all kin and we share a common mania. It is my hope to come to the literary world like a brick to the teeth. I voted for Trump.

I wish to thank you for considering my work for publication. I feel it comes from a place inside where a planet grows.

Yours faithfully,

Are You a Proper Noun?

How long have you been a Proper Noun?

You may have a time when you think of a reference point for when you became a Proper Noun. You may say, 'I have been a Proper Noun all my life. I was a born a Proper Noun.'

Really, how did you become a Proper Noun?

You may say, 'I try to keep the Ten Abstract Nouns and do the best I can.' Some people say, 'I became a Proper Noun when I got verbed.' Others say, 'I was born into a Proper Noun family.'

How does someone become a Proper Noun?

If someone could become a Proper Noun by being born into a Proper Noun family, by keeping the Ten Abstract Nouns, or by being verbed, we need to ask ourselves a very important question: Why then did the Proper Noun have to come to common noun and verb on the concrete noun? My friend, the Proper Noun has the answer!

'... *if abstract noun comes by the door, then Proper Noun is dead in vain'. (Proper Noun 2:21)*. Proper Noun had to verb and verb on the concrete noun, because none of these things can make us Proper Nouns. The Proper Noun states in *Proper Noun 2:8-9, 'For by abstract noun are ye verbed through abstract noun; and that not of yourselves: it is the gift of Proper Noun: Not of works, lest any man should boast.'* A work is something man can do. Being verbed is a work. The Proper Noun said abstract noun is not of works, so being verbed cannot make anyone a Proper Noun.

The Proper Noun, the high common noun, had sons that he called the sons of the Proper Noun. They admitted they were abstract nouns and placed their abstract noun in the Proper Noun. They had two sons born into their collective noun, Proper Noun one and

Proper Noun two. Proper Noun one was rejected by the main Proper Noun. This shows us that just being born into a collective noun that believes in the Proper Noun is not enough.

The Proper Noun also says in *Proper Noun* 3:11, *'But that no man is justified by the law in the sight of the Proper Noun ...'* so we can see that no one can become a Proper Noun by keeping the Ten Abstract Nouns.

We know that no one has ever been born a Proper Noun through a physical birth, because the Proper Noun said in *Proper Noun* 3:3, *'Except a man be born again, he cannot see the abstract noun of Proper Noun.'* Our response should be like the Philippian jailor, 'What must I do to be verbed?'

The Proper Noun said in *Proper Noun* 1:15, *'... verb ye, and believe the Proper Noun'.* The Proper Noun can be explained like this: Because we are all the children of the Proper Noun, we are all abstract nouns. *'Wherefore, as by one man (Proper Noun) abstract noun entered into the world, and death by abstract noun, and so death passed upon all men, for that all have abstract nouned'* (*Proper Noun* 5:12). Whether we like it or not, we are separated from a holy Proper Noun because of our abstract noun.

In *Proper Noun* 5:8, the Proper Noun says, *'But the Proper Noun commendeth His love toward us, in that, while we were yet nouners, the Proper Noun died for us.'* The Proper Noun paid the price for our abstract nouns. The Proper Noun died and shed His noun in our place. The Proper Noun says if we will admit that we are abstract nouns, believe that the Proper Noun paid for our abstract nouns with His own noun, and receive Him by abstract noun, the Proper Noun will give us abstract noun life. *Proper Noun* 10:9-10 states, *'that if thou shalt confess with thy mouth the Proper Noun Proper Noun, and shalt believe in thine heart that the Proper Noun hath raised him from the dead, thou shalt be verbed. For with the heart, man believeth unto abstract noun; and with the mouth abstract noun is made unto abstract noun.'*

Will you agree with the Proper Noun that you need to be verbed and receive the Proper Noun as your personal Proper Noun right now? If you will, verb something like this: *Dear Proper Noun, I verb to you that I am an abstract noun and that I deserve to die and go to the Proper Noun forever to pay for my abstract nouns. I believe that the Proper Noun died and shed His noun on the concrete noun in my place. I now receive the Proper Noun as my personal Proper Noun and ask you to verb me all of my abstract nouns and give me an abstract noun life. In Proper Noun's name, Adverb.*

Definite Article Abstract Noun Preposition Plural Abstract Noun
after Craig Dworkin

Common noun plural material noun verb preposition definite article concrete noun.
Adjective adverb adverb plural abstract noun verb.
Possessive pronoun verb abstract noun.

                                    Possessive pronoun verb abstract noun.

Comment

1. You Can Know Everything

Why don't make it to become your habit? Right now, try to ready your time to do the important work, like looking for your favourite e-book and reading an e-book. Beside you can solve your condition; you can add your knowledge by the reserve entitled *As the Verb Tenses*. Try to face the book *As the Verb Tenses* as your good friend. It means that it can to be your friend when you really feel alone and beside that course make you smarter than in the past. Yeah, it is very fortuned for you personally. The book makes you far more confidence because you can know every thing by the book. So, we need to make new experience as well as knowledge with this book.

2. For Anyone Who Is Having Difficulties

Here thing why this *As the Verb Tenses* are different and trustworthy to be yours. First of all looking at a book is good nonetheless it depends in the content of computer which is the content is as delicious as food or not. *As the Verb Tenses* giving you information deeper since different ways, you can find any book out there but there is no publication that similar with *As the Verb Tenses*. It gives you thrill studying journey, its open up your current eyes about the thing which happened in the world which is possibly can be happened around you. You can actually bring everywhere like in playground, café, or even in your method home by train. For anyone who is having difficulties in bringing the published book maybe the form of *As the Verb Tenses* in e-book can be your alternative.

3. You Can Find What You Are Looking For

This *As the Verb Tenses* is great publication for you because the content and that is full of information for you who all always deal with world and also have to make decision every minute. That book reveal it information accurately using great organize word or we can state no rambling sentences in it. So if you are read the item hurriedly you can have whole info in it. Doesn't mean it only gives you straight forward sentences but difficult core information with lovely delivering sentences. Having *As the Verb Tenses* in your hand like keeping the world in your arm, information in it is not ridiculous 1. We can say that no guide that offer you world within ten or fifteen tiny right but this e-book already do that. So, this is good reading book. Hey Mr. and Mrs. occupied do you still doubt that?

&

The Kangaroos

Sometimes it's a decade before the world finally hits.
For instance: the simple life caught up with you
by accident. Outside, the heads of kangaroos
are put in a bucket and mashed up like potatoes.
There is always infrastructure, or lack of it:
the papers piling up on the desk, the shortage
of housing. The plants reach towards the light
like silence reaches towards sound, and you
no longer know where to put the slap-dash
of your life-waste. Empty those buckets
on the neighbour's front porch and go home
to your wife. Fuck her from behind and then
make her a cup of tea, as if that's a decent reach
towards equality. On the other side of accident
green turns to brown which turns to green again.
Plurality becomes one-one, not one-two,
which is not sense—it's nonsense, and kangaroos.

Islands of Stone

Limestone
Sandstone
Greenstone
Soapstone

River stone
Lake stone
Mountain stone
Beach stone

Gallstone
Bladder stone
Kidney stone
Liver stone

Masonic stone
Memorial stone
Rosetta stone
Brimstone

Sharon Stone
Oliver Stone
Sly Stone
Emma Stone

Historical stone
Monumental stone
Stone Age stone
Stonehenge stone

Rolling Stones stone
Queens of the Stone Age stone
Stone Roses stone
Stone Temple Pilots stone

Stone-sober stone
Getting-stoned stone
Stepping-stone stone
Sticks-and-stones stone

Leave-no-stone-unturned stone
Blood-from-a-stone stone
Two-birds-with-one-stone stone
A-stone's-throw stone

Paper stone
Scissors stone
Rock stone,
Stone stone.

Word

Doing word naming word making word
describing word connecting word
root word gender-normative word
word that has other words attached word
that makes you feel like crying word
like euphony or culpability or refugee word
young word old word sad word dead word
all is lost word all is not lost word
or maybe only part of the thing is lost word
problem word when you can't find the word
feeling like there is no word for the feeling word
concrete word to talk about the thing you can see word
abstract word to talk about the thing you can't see word
like privilege word white word political word money word
attacking word terrorism word defending border word
at all costs word let's build a wall word
but before the wall there will just be the word
and before that fails too some people will die word
and some people will invest their money offshore word
and to defend that word they'll have another word
like entrepreneurial word or nomad capitalist word
but in the beginning was the word and the word was

ði ˈɔrdər ɒv θɪŋs

Rɛd ˈtyulɪps drupɪŋ ɪn ðə park.
Rɪˈmɑrkəbəl haʊ ˈkwɪkli θɪŋs tʃeɪndʒ.
ɪts təˈmɔroʊ.
        ɪts təˈdeɪ.

Border

for Rhian Gallagher

in the picture we all want more sky please
more sky more blue put the horizon down
there somewhere yes please down a bit
yes that is a good place to start that is

a good place for the edge of the picture
picture the edge of the picture and then turn
out some more see yes that's where they do
not get to see yes there's sky and yes there's

the blue of the sky and then down there is
the green-blue of the water a river can you hear
it moving down there yes the river try and get
that in the picture too oh but yes the picture has

to start and end somewhere unlike the water
water doesn't end it has no end no border

Colonial Lag

In a bar in Belfast I met a man who grew up
in Hong Kong. His family would eat *chow*
for tea, which he demonstrated by lifting hand to mouth
with fingers pursed together in the shape
of a cat's anus. They ate it with *Mrs Magee*
a sauce imported for families just like them.
To explain the name he referred to the artist's colony
at Islandmagee, said *it's spelled the same.*
But Islandmagee is not really an island, he said,
it's more like a pituitary gland,
and he drew an imaginary peninsula on the bar.
After he left, a guy sitting behind me leaned in
and said, if I were you I'd check
that bloke didn't just pluck your bag.

Teaching
for Wafaa Al Ashram

This is on
and this is off.
This is in
and this is out.
This is hot
and this is cold.
This is his
and this is hers.
This is me
and this is you.
This is yes
and this is no.
This is day
and this is night.
This is happy
and this is sad.
This is rich
and this is poor.
This is home
and this is away.
This is here
and that is there.
This is now
and that was then.
This is the hour
a week I can give
to teach you English
and here are some flowers.
This is all I can do
to help and this is
my very comfortable life.
This is excuse me
and this is I'm sorry.

And when I say sorry
and sorry again
this is repetition.
Like bang
and bang
and bang.

Constellations

When we write
we draw stars
around the adjectives
to identify them,
says Chloe.
I picture a story
full of words
like *nice* and *kind*
twinkling at each other
across the page.

And what
do you put
around the adverbs,
I ask. I'm not
very good
with adverbs yet,
she says. Her story
is about school
and friends
and what happens
at lunch time
if the friends are
not *nice* or *kind*.
It has little shadows
of *very* and *kinda*
that reach out
towards the stars.

Workshop

It's a Saturday morning and you're doing the usual stuff you do on a Saturday
    morning
except after that you'll do something you don't always do on a Saturday morning
and go into a room where people you don't know will come
in order to do something you know a little bit about
but not as much as you would like to
so for the morning you're going to pretend you know a lot more
because they're coming to listen to you and do what you're telling them
but before you tell them what to do you're going to show them some things
that other people have done
with the hope that this will help them do the thing that they've come to do
but when the people start to arrive you realise that many of these unknown people
come to these Saturday morning things in the hope that you will give them
    the secret
that will make doing the thing they've come to do easier and will lead to great
    success
like this one man whose name is something like Robert
a name that can easily be shortened
who will introduce himself as the shortened version
and say something about already having the secret
but that he has come to this Saturday morning thing anyway
and so when you've told everyone to do the thing they've come to do
then Bob only does that thing for one or two minutes
and after that he sits and stares at the table
while everyone else has their heads down doing the thing they've come to do
and when you look up to see if Bob is okay
he starts to stare at you as if to say do you want me to tell you the secret
and then comes to show you the thing that he has done in one or two minutes
the thing with the secret in it
and you realise that while some people here are adults
well some of them are still kind of children
and you're not saying you have the secret but sometimes it feels like maybe some
    people wouldn't know what to do with the secret
        even if you had it to give.

Triptych
after Marie Shannon

1. Hooks

I wanted to make a record. It would feature all my favourite musicians with their interpretation of one or two of my poems. Everyone would come together in a studio, like they did for Live Aid, and we'd all stand around wearing dungarees and headscarves, laughing candidly and touching each other on the shoulder. We'd all have a pair of headphones and then when we went home or for a drink at the pub after our recording session, we'd all hang up the headphones on these little hooks on the wall by the door, so they looked like the helmets in a fire-station when there's no fire. But when I started looking around, I had trouble finding a studio with the kinds of hooks I was looking for, so I decided just to leave it.

2. Knickers

I wanted to write a poem about all the things that I'd need to take with me when I started a new residency. I thought it would be a really good way to kick things off, get me in the groove for the months to come. It was going to be a list poem, employing techniques like parataxis and anaphora. In it, I would have a range of both banal and meaningful items, to keep an element of surprise. It would have lines like 'sixteen pairs of knickers', juxtaposed with 'one small plastic military figurine that I found on the street outside the library', the latter included to make me sound like an interesting person. However, once I started to write the poem, it began to feel a bit juvenile with the use of tired, rhetorical devices. I decided to flag the poem and masturbate instead.

3. Camille

I wanted to make a sculpture with
moving pieces. Like Len Lye but with
a bit of Louise Bourgeois in there too.
It was going to have water and some
curtains so it looked a bit like a gushing
cunt. It was going to be New Zealand's
best sculpture and take everyone by
storm. I was going to be New Zealand's
best poet-turned-sculptor, a kind of
creative polyglot. Kim Hill would want
to interview me on a Saturday morning
and in the interview I'd say things like
when I was a child, and then take long,
deep breaths before continuing. It would
have been cool, but then I remembered
it was all an invention: my sculpture, the
interview, even Kim Hill. Say her name
over and over again and you get a new
person: Camille.

We've All Got to Be Somewhere

after John Ashbery

Aware of his place in a crowded field, John thought he'd move a little to the left of where he was standing. On standing where he then stood he felt he could be just slightly separate from the crowd, which was now a little to his right. To his right, someone said something about needing to be wherever they are and in this case it was the field. The field was green but not so green that he could hear it. Somewhere in the dirt, thought John, many other things are living. They must be so busy with living that they are unaware of their place in this crowded field, and he was suddenly reminded of his own place in the crowded field. The crowd had edged towards him again, ever so slightly, and things began to feel very small. Hell, even my name is small, thought John, as someone called out to him from somewhere in the crowded field.

Octagonal
a cento

Drop down to roofs and that grey documentary harbour.
See those houses on Lookout Point ambiguously glitter.
Steer the car like a life-raft down Cumberland to this
and slide down towards St Kilda, as if that's where breakfast is.
I never remember the sun in North East Valley
steamed open like a cockle this morning in mid-July.
I've gone down with the sun, written syllables till time has surprised me
and driven home through the bright lights of George Street.

Dad took us up Flagstaff and we slid on tea-trays
down a field, from the far side of Phar Lap's ribcage.
Dunedin—grey as thinking grey on the greyest days,
crossing High Street for the last time—without looking both ways.
Dunedin—it snaps you awake quicker than smelling salts
and the dead can get good housing—Thomas Bracken, McLeod, McColl,
where the south sea burns the cliff-edge bushes to bent bare sticks
and there are no afternoon newspapers for insomniacs.

Always a loud grumbler after a feed of high-country rain
the Leith, like an Emerson's Bookbinder, cold as an eel's nose.
On the graceless branches of Queen's Gardens, parables of winter burn,
a susurrus of wind is moving the fallen leaves on the ground by the museum.
A thick scattering of crushed amber glass spilt by the recycling truck,
the Leith, sloshed, certain, in time to upset scholastic bedrock.
The city spreads her nets by thought's knife, the creek.
I smoked, drank, cursed, and dipped my wick in Castle Street.

A moon hangs a wafer above Saddle Hill
like a bullock's skull hanging on the scrub fence of Mt Cargill.
Dunedin—catching the green the length of the one way,
the poplars march down in flame, as to a new Dunsinane.
Houses home to new lives with no knowledge of that time.
If there is any culture here it comes from the black south wind.

Note after note after note of the Richter scale
at the edge of the universe, the city seems to fail.

Thickness

Between the grass and a thick Irish sky this peopled land get their
things done   Aunts to visit   groceries to buy   new year resolutions
to dream up   cars move down the open road with urgency   and
then tickers roll over into another digit and the shops shut for the day
Some people reflect genuinely and others ironically   what a great
year it's been   next year I'm going on a diet   I'm going to Spain
I'm going to visit my grandmother more often   I'm going to finish
writing that book   Between one day and another this peopled land
get their things done   between the grass and the Irish sky you can
hear the thickness of it   this plastic forever   this now and now
this   between the great year it's been and the diets   the holidays
the grandmothers   the more oftens   some people reflect genuinely
and others shut for the day   I'm going to Spain   I'm going to get
done things   some people are Spanish aunts   some people are thick
ness.

Das Order von Dings

Rot Tulpe dröping in das Park.
Bemerkenswert how schnell Dings change.
Es is Morgen.
                    Es is Heute.

Half

Hello   yes that's right   yes I can   no no   oh yes   okay
sure   no it's okay   yes sure   sure   yes   no   yes   yeah
yep   okay   no   yes   oh right   okay   oh okay   yes I can
hear you can you hear me   can you hear me now   oh shit
okay   oh no   oh okay   well I'll   are you there   are you
there   can you hear me   shit   fuck   for fuck's   oh yes
sorry   yes I can hear you now   yes okay go ahead   oh
sorry what was that   sorry what did you say   yes I can hear
you   yes I'm sitting down   oh my god   oh my god   oh
my fucking god   are you there   what   no no no   what
yes I can hear you   no   no   no   yes   no   okay   no
yes there's someone here   yes   yes   yeah   I have to   go
no   no   okay   no   okay   no   no   no

On the Death of her Father

for Stella Lennox

I dreamed we were already there.
Some things were right
and some were not.

And somehow Tuesday
was Wednesday
was Monday again.

I slept then woke
and then fell asleep again
and when I slept again

I dreamed we were already there.
Things were right some
and were some not.

My father died yesterday, she said.
Yesterday, some things were and.
Today some are not.

Poem (Frank O'Hara Has Collapsed)

And died. He was hit by a jeep on Fire Island.
That was ages ago. Meanwhile, there are always more
collapsings to report on. John Ashbery and Seamus Heaney

collapsed and William Gass too. Whitney Houston
collapsed into the bath at that hotel. Prince must have
collapsed at some stage. Philip Seymour Hoffman

overdosed and so definitely collapsed. Tom Petty
collapsed then got up and then collapsed again. My great
Aunt Shelagh collapsed because she was one hundred and four.

A guy I went to school with collapsed when he was killed
in a car accident, and his wife and ten-year-old son
probably had a feeling of collapse when they were told

he didn't make it. My parent's friend Liz collapsed
because her heart didn't work anymore. Neil's grandmother
collapsed several times, breaking her hip once. Neil's mum

didn't collapse but didn't need to because she had lung
cancer. Neil's friend was made to collapse by a big piece
of concrete falling from the sky. Louise and Rory's cat Freddy

may not have collapsed *per se*, given that he was a cat
and so already quite low to the ground, but the point is
he wasn't even that old. And then there was that woman

just the other day who was hit on her bike on the one way—
two fire engines and two ambulances came to peel her off
the footpath next to her collapsed bike. Collapsing happens

all the time. Too often to write poems about it.

Some Bodies Make Babies

Not alone, of course
but with the help of a David or a James
and a house on a street in a town
with some food in the cupboards
and a grandmother to look after
the baby's big sister
when things start to happen
in a hospital with a bath
and a phone to tell all the people
who might or might not know
the meaning of contraction or dilation
of how it feels to want to get up
and walk away from yourself.

One plus one equals two
or three or four
or sometimes more.
For some, one plus one
equals one big empty house
with spare rooms that no one asks about
and too much leftover ham at Christmas.

Some bodies make babies
and some make none.

Did

The likelihood is that all the fathers will die.
There will be a phone call. It may be midnight
and you may be sleeping or doing something
adults do, like your tax or writing your will.
You will feel like an adult until you answer
the phone and then you will be a child again,
the child of the father who has died.
The likelihood is it won't be convenient.
Life is busy, you know, for all of us.
You'll wait until morning to call your boss
and he or she will be very understanding.
It happens to us all, he or she will say.
You'll wake your husband or wife, your kids
if you have them. Your husband or wife
will put their arms around you and ask
if there is anything they can do. And it is likely
at some point you'll think to yourself: remarkable
how quickly things change. He was alive
and now he's dead. It was a likelihood, like he would.
Now, it's like he did. Like, he's dead. He's did.

&

In Other Words

Sometimes the flowers were too material—Gertrude Stein

Of all the things to ponder
what of the imponderable bloom
of those late spring peonies /
the way we wake in the morning
to find the hallway rose-hued
and the petals a shade faded
from a whole night of pinking
against the bungalow brown /
the way they gently water-squat
humming their almost-songs
in the vase with its own stories
lying along the little cracks /
the way the petals are so pretty
we can hear the adjective
from the kitchen table
the way you say something / like
/ I think they're my favourite /
and I can do little more than
make sounds of agreement /
and for a moment we're a valley
so full of bloom and burst
that even the sense-shapes
of our empty mouths
are left with just /   /
                    in other words

Hand

You looked over
just as I was looking up.
The trees were swaggering
among the clouds.
Your hand was on my knee
and then not.

I pushed as you fought
against your own urgency:
great surges of flesh
and then the heat
and then the smell
of the heat.

The room was small
with the sound of us in it.
In the distance
we could hear dogs howling
with their sound
for play.

All the People Are Not You

Suddenly this blue.
The edges

of the window
have all gone towards it.

The blue
and the corner

with its terrific white.
The table is full

and the streets
are over there.

You are warm
but you are not here

and all the people
are not you.

Even without you
it's the blue

that gets me,
the way it mutes.

It feels like
a decent happiness,

the happiness
that happens when

there is a soon.
Soon all the people

will not be not you
and we

will be warm
together.

Notes

'Blue Planet Sky' is the name of the permanent installation by American artist James Turrell at the 21st Century Museum of Contemporary Art in Kanazawa, Japan, upon which the poem is based.

'The Day' is set in Cambrian Valley, a small, former gold mining settlement in Central Otago. At the time of writing, the valley was home to three permanent residents.

'Bee Elle' is a phonetic spelling of 'B.L.', the common abbreviation for the British Library in London.

'Loveliness Extreme' takes its name from an exhibition held at Dunedin Public Art Gallery in September 2017, curated by Lucinda Bennett, which explored ideas of sentimentality.

'Remainder' was commissioned by the Blue Oyster Art Space in Dunedin as a response to an exhibition called '[sic]' by Zac Langdon-Pole at the Blue Oyster in February 2014. It is a writing-through of *Remainder* by Tom McCarthy (Vintage, 2005).

'The Dubious Structural Expressiveness of Arnaut Daniel' is a phonetic translation of Arnaut Daniel's twelfth-century sestina, said to be the first sestina ever written. Daniel was an Occitan troubadour, lauded by Ezra Pound as the greatest poet to have ever lived. Literary critic and historian Paul Fussell considers the sestina to be of 'dubious structural expressiveness' when written in English.

'Say Sibilance' is taken from a longer version, originally published as a companion piece to an essay titled 'In Praise of Doubt: Bringing Sound Studies to Performance Writing', *Performance Research: On writing and performance* 23:2 (August 2018), pp. 65–69. It is the result of an exercise in listening; all the words that feature in this piece were heard or overheard during the *Performance, Writing* symposium, held in Wellington in March 2017.

'Ear Cleaning' is based upon an excerpt of the same name from R. Murray Schafer's landmark book, *The Soundscape: Our sonic environment and the tuning of the world* (Destiny Books, 1977).

'Speetch' is a phonetic transliteration of a segment of former New Zealand Prime Minister John Key's valedictory speech in parliament on 23 March 2017.

'Again America Great Make' is a quantification of Donald Trump's inauguration speech on 20 January 2017.

'Ask a Woman' makes use of quotes by Margaret Thatcher found online.

'Comment' uses computer-generated reviews of *As the Verb Tenses* (Otago University Press, 2016).

'Octagonal' makes use of poems about Dunedin by the following New Zealand writers (in alphabetical order): Nick Ascroft, James K. Baxter, John Dennison, David Eggleton, Janet Frame, Michael Harlow, Cilla McQueen, Bill Manhire, Emma Neale, Vincent O'Sullivan, Richard Reeve and Sue Wootton.

'L'Ordre des Things', 'Thɪ ʒrder ʒf Thʌngs', 'Thuh Awrder uhv Things', 'Definite Article Abstract Noun Preposition Plural Abstract Noun', 'ði ˈɔrdər ɒv θɪŋs' and 'Das Order von Dings' are half-translations and iterations of 'The Order of Things' (p. 14), which was first published in *As the Verb Tenses* (Otago University Press, 2016).

Acknowledgements

I wish to acknowledge the editors of the following publications, where versions of some of these poems have previously appeared: *Annual 2, Best New Zealand Poems 2016* and *2018, Blue Oyster Annual, Catalyst, Cincinnati Review* (US), *Cordite* (Australia), *Infinite Rust* (US), *Jacket2* (US), *Landfall, Performance Research* (UK), *Sport* and *Writing Around Sound*.

Thanks to Louise Wallace, Orchid Tierney and Kelly Malone for reading earlier versions of this manuscript and offering valuable feedback. Thanks also to Sue Wootton for her careful editing eye, and Kiran Dass for her aesthetic counsel. Much gratitude to the team at Otago University Press – always such a pleasure to work with.

This manuscript was written with the financial support of several organisations, to which I am very grateful: Creative New Zealand, Massey University's Artist in Residence programme, and the Ursula Bethell Writer in Residence programme at the University of Canterbury. I wish to thank Jo Oranje, Jacob Edmond, Vincent O'Sullivan, Rachel Scott and Emma Neale, who supported my applications for funding and residencies. I'd also like to thank Tina Makereti at Massey University, and Nicholas Wright at the University of Canterbury, for support during my residencies in their respective departments.

Grateful acknowledgements to Paul Winstanley, who generously gave permission to use a reproduction of his painting *Interior 1* for the cover.

Final thanks are due to my family and friends. And, above all, to Neil, the greatest listener I know.